SUNSETS AND ORCHIDS

BY THE WRITERS OF INDIA

THE DIVINE PUBLICATIONS

Contents

Contents

Acknowledgements

Firstly, we would like to express our gratitude to our brilliant compilers SWALEHA AMEER and SAMAN AHMAD for their hardwork. Without them this book would not have become a reality.

Our special thanks to the whole team for their constant support and their valuable suggestions.

We would like to express our gratitude to our talented authors for becoming a part of this book with their beautiful work.

The Divine Publications

Instagram: @the_divinepublications

1. JUHI PATHAK

Juhi Pathak is a 19 years old word-compiler from Bareilly, U.P. with a passion of expressing her thoughts via words. She has penned over 800 poems in English, Hindi, French, Spanish and Greek.

Black Orchids

I have a simple request—
can we please speak in flowers?
It'll be much easier to talk to the hearts
without our verbal powers.
And if we fail to comprehend
and end up losing our track,
we can always exchange orchids
that are painted in pure black.
Black orchids, you might think,
seem to radiate heavy gloom;
but my darling, do you see
the way they cordially bloom?
No other colour can match
the warmth black orchids hold
and none can possess their

coldness too that's arctic as gold.
To consider, no other can carry
the love black orchids bring;
and none can pack in themselves
cruel hatred for something.
Where can you expect to find
such a cosmic concoction
if not in a bouquet,
given that it is an ebonized black one?

2. SHRIPARNA NANDI

I am a budding writer from West Bengal, India. It all started with writing two liners and now I've ended up to this. I don't want to stop here but dream of achieving big in future.

How do you define Love?

Love is strange; falling head over heels
Love is confusing; of not having the same feels
Love is complicated, love is different, it's not always an Adam and Eve affair be it one sided or unrequited, Love in all kinds is fair.
Love is freedom to express who you are No judgements, no insecurities, a medicine to all scars.
Love is a feeling of a spirit untamed, of your heart beating fast from your chest.
Love is the battle , if you should or shouldn't, put your arms around her waist.
Love is mystic, love is bold ; alluring through the deep folds of heart spitting out those golden words is also an art.
But, sometimes, love can hurt, it can be heavy Love troubles, love breaks but also mends and binds.
Love is tender, love is sweet, hard to find.

Love is the kindness that beholds the world, a thread that unites
to summarise the feelings,
Love is what fire does to ice.

3. NANDINI KARMAKAR

Nandini Karmakar is currently pursuing her bachelor's from DU. She loves to write poems. She has written 25 poems till now and will write many more soon. Her poems have been published in 10 anthologies in total. She believes that we all have hidden talents waiting to be discovered. We just have to work on it.

TAKE ME BACK

Take me to the time, when there was no fear,
Take me to the time, when I talked, everyone just heard.
Take me to the time, when I had only good friends,
Take me to the time, when I didn't know to pretend.
Take me to the time, when I only ate, slept and played
Take me to the time, when I was happy every single day.
Take me to the time, when I had nothing to lose,
All I cared was about my school, parents and friends.
Take me back to those golden days,
Take me back to those good old days.
Take me back to my childhood, take me back to my childhood.

4. KRIPALI MAKHECHA

Kripali is from Gujarat. She is passionate about reading and writing since her childhood. She likes to help people with their emotional and mental health issues and she always tries to learn something new from life.

BEAUTY HUNT

Three person went for their trip in one old village between mountains. They took two rooms in hotel: one for couple and one for their friend. They roam everywhere in the village on the first day. At night, they were sitting in a garden and a watchman came. They all were curious to know about that beautiful village so they asked the old watchman. He told all the interesting stories about village, At last, man asked about the mountain beside village. The watchman got scared, stood up and started going. He said while going, "sir, don't ever look at that mountain in your life". They stopped him and asked again and again about mountain. They were surprised how he got scared by the name of mountain.

After some efforts, he started narrating the story.

Few years ago, there was a rumour in village about a witch living on that mountain. Some guys who showed her was describing her as a scary old lady. Suddenly, girls started missing in that village. people gathered and went to that witch's house because they had a doubt over the witch in missing report of girls. When they saw her, their doubt came true. She was a beautiful young lady with pretty eyes as one missing girl, brown long hair as another missing girl, lips and another body parts were looking like other missing girls. When she used to like something in a girl. She would kidnapp them and transfer their body parts in her. By this way she could live young and pretty. People warned her and came back. For few days, there was peace in village.

After few days, another girl got missing. People were sure but they wanted a proof for taking any serious action. One guy said at that moment, when they went to witch's house he noticed that witch didn't have left toe and the foot prints gained from missing girl's house also didn't have left toe. Then, they went to witch's home again, tied her with one tree and burned her alive. From that day, if a girl or lady went over that mountain died because of witch's curse and when they die their one body part would be missing. So no one would go to that mountain. Watchman left for his house and guys were still there talking about that mountain. They thought, people of this village are so superstitious because they went to that mountain that day only and they were all alive and safe. At late night, they went to sleep. During last duration young man who was sleeping with his wife heard one voice of counting numbers.

He thought his wife was counting money, so he asked her to sleep and count money the next morning but but the voice didn't stop. After some time it reach to 50 thousand above. The man realised that they didn't have that much money. He woke up from sleep and looked everywhere. He went close to that side of room from where voice was coming. There stood a scary old lady as described by the watchman. Her wife was dead and the witch was picking and counting her hair. Man got unconscious. The next morning ,when he gained consciousness he saw police and people in his room. Her wife was dead and her dead body didn't have any hair on head.

5. SINDHU REDDY

Sindhu Reddy is the author of" TWO BULLETS COLLIDE. "
She is a nineteen-year-old avid reader and writer. She strives to
make an impact through her writings. Insta- sindhu.author
It doesn't matter
how wealthy you are,
how famous you are,
how greedy you are,
how guilty you are,
how sad you are,
how jealous you are on your death bed.
Because what matters is, are you content and grateful for living
your life?
If yes, then you will rest in peace.
If not, you will crave for time which ticked off while you were
crawling for worldly desires.
So live life profoundly.

6. AAYUSH DUBEY

Aayush Dubey is a student who is pursuing a Bachelor's Degree from the university of Allahabad. He is 18 years old and loves to write poems and quotes. Writing is very close to his heart, he loves to express himself through his work. He hopes to do something great in the field of writing and maybe someday people will admire him and his work. In short, Aayush is an optimistic being who wants to become an ideal for the next generation.

A monster is present neath every human,
Or humans are monsters using masks to hide their truth.
A monster who wants himself happy and others' pain doesn't matter to him.
A monster who is hungry for money and all the fame.
A monster who makes everyone sad, a monster who never gets failed.
A monster is a human atop, a human is a monster who never stops.

7. SAMIKSHA RAVINDRA WAGHMARE

Hello, my name is Samiksha Ravindra Waghmare. I am a college student. I Like to write poems, stories,like reading and sketching. My happiness is in writing poems.

WINGS

Wings in my lines, Feelings is my shines words in my lines, to gives me a power of my strength.
Wings in my lines, Feelings is my shines. Lines touched my heart, words catch my mind.
Wings in my lines, Feelings is my shines. Things are touchable, Wings are flyable. Sky is blue, My mind is flu.
Wings in my lines, Feelings is my shines. Love is a peace of my feelings, Pain felt me in a guilty.
Wings in my lines, Feelings is my shines. Don't worry, Don't worry
Wings in my lines, Feelings is my shines.

8. PAYAL JAISWAL

She is payal jaiswal from Kushinagar, Uttar Pradesh. She is done with her graduation and now doing masters in political science. Her parents are very much supportive in nature andencourage her to persue what she wants. The best part about her is the love to work for charity. She has been a co-author of 15+ anthologys .Best way to connect with her is through Insta I'd -@payaljais2181 and also can reach out at payaljaiswal419@gmail.com

She is a girl, that's why she is asked to speak less , she is asked to bear everything silently.

I thought that she will get respect like men in society, but no news there was a shadow and there will be deep darkness in her life. what a girl she is just because whenever she wanted to make her dreams come true, her dreams were broken and she was shaped like a piece of glass.

Instead of books in her hands the burden of the housewife was given when she stepped in the homely life, She was taken by the society to expect the qualities , she was killed, she was burnt for dowry, there is still time to recognize the nature's precious creation, otherwise one day the structure of this universe will be spoiled. You will crave for the love of a mother, daughter, sister,lover and one day you will curse your own nature.

9. SRIJA SADHUKHAN

Srija Sadhukhan is studying BSc Biotechnology in Amity University Kolkata. Lovesto write poetry and a book worm too. Few years ago, pain arrived silently in my life. Entered in my heart without knocking. Hurt me day and night witha knife, burned me with those past memories. During those days, every night became my strength. Somehow I fell in love with pain, When it wanted to leave my heart. I held him back and asked it to stay back. Now a days, Pain became usual to my heart. But then I got tired. So, I asked pain to leave me alone.

FAR AWAY FROM REALITY

Pen:- "Are you okay?"

Me:- "ya!!"

Pen:- "Really??"

Me :- "no just kidding"

Pen:- "I know you will again write your sad feelings and then you will start crying "

Me:- "Not at all! I am not a kid anymore"

Pen:- " Really! Then two days back you were a kid and now you grown up, right?"

Me:- "Mmmmm. Actually not. I have moved on."

Pen:- *"That's like my girl. I know you can do it. And see you did it?"*

Me:- *" Actually there is no one who understands me the way you do, I mean like the way you encourage me and make me laugh".*

Pen:- *"Really? Uff, atleast you think I have some importance in your life?"*

Me:- *"Of course yes, infinite yes, my love. You add stability to my life. I can share everything with you. Thank you"*

Pen:- *"Stop this drama, ha, so need of this formalities. And one more think, start your work again, my love, I will always be with you. "*

Me:-*" So let's start, I wish our friendship never ends and stays like this forever, right?"*

Pen:-*" Did you watch any film before returning home?"*

Me:-*" No, why?"*

Pen:-*" I fear that you are using tooooo much filmy dialogues man, it's ok. I will always be with you whatever may be the situation. And the memories will be created forever".*

Me:-*"Filmy haa. Ok. Love you dumbo".*

Pen:- *"Love you too my drama queen. Whenever you need my help just share the things with me".*

Me:-*"I will, aah , I feel good now. Fresh and happy".*

Pen:-*" I know you will, those memories of us and our friendship will always be a refresh moment. "*

Me:- *"Yeah".*

10. BHAVYA RAWAT

I am a high school junior, nature enthusiast and a avid reader. I live in Dehradun. I love literature and hope to do higher studies in it. I mostly write poem on nature.

THE KNOWN UNKNOWN HUMAN ADDICTION

Human pluck the flowers, showing how addicted they are to beautiful things;
In a similar way, humans pluck the kind humans.

11. ISHITA MEHAL

Currently a student, I'm trying to understand how the world works. I passionately write about feelings while petting four kittens, my only friends.

TAKE A DEEP BREATHE

Take a deep breathe Watch the smoke wreathe You and the endless sky Don't ask why Let go of all inhibitions Slyly immerse in your imagination Forget the world around Wish to be never found Or slip into slumber Reminisce when you were younger Weave those memories And keep it till centuries Detach from the present Only for a moment Then you'll get a surprise Before opening you eyes Take a deep breathe Watch the smoke wreathe You and the endless sky Don't ask why

Article - "There is nothing either good or bad but thinking makes it so". The great author William Shakespeare once philosophized on the essence of life's beauty through his famous play "Hamlet". He wrote that "There is nothing good or bad, only thinking makes it so". Shakespeare was truly a genius and his work on literature has an ever-shining coat of eternity. There is no universal standard as to what is good or bad. We were not born with laws inscribed on our body. So, who decides what is good or bad? It is our thinking alone? And what influences our thinking? What we think is right or wrong is all in our head, and it enters our head because of what society teaches us. T teaches us. To elaborate, I think that our idea and interpretation of good or bad is inextricably intertwined with our upbringing, cultural backgrounds, internal biases, pre conceived notions and experiences. It is our thinking and perception that paves way to our life but they are shaped and influenced vastly/greatly by the society and to some extent also by the people we live and interact with. The society is the one that creates an atmosphere, or alters the situation and reshapes it to a set default, which may or may not be correct in all aspects. Certain events are classified as good or bad by the behaviour of the majority of the population. It denotes the majority opinion, and that is not necessarily good or right. Human beings are social animals who live and grow with the society, so irrespective of if we admit it or not, we surely do care for the public opinion and let our minds think in a similar manner. We label certain events as good and others as bad because we have been tau

because we have been taught from a young age to differentiate good from bad. Our deep-rooted learning since childhood goes to our sub-conscious mind which gets projected out through our thinking. But good or bad is subjective in nature. What is good in one society, in one age, in one pattern of culture, may be bad in another. What is considered good for one person can be bad for another. Like people talk about a glass of water half-filled differently. Some people see the glass with a touch of 'positivity and optimism', calling it as 'half full' while the other group sees it with a touch of 'negativity and pessimism' calling it as 'half empty'. Both describe the status of the glass with some water correctly. Then what explains the different viewpoints of appreciation and depreciation of the glass? It is our thinking. A single situation varies drastically for two different people. No two people are same. Everyone differs in their behaviour and mannerism.

mannerism. For some success is becoming rich and famous whereas for some it is to lead a comfortable life fulfilling basic needs. For one failure means an end but for another it's an opportunity to learn and become better. In fact, contradictions and dichotomies exist even within ourselves. We are neither entirely good nor completely bad but simply human beings. There is a curious mixture of good and bad in us which is determined by various intricacies and complexities. We humans have been gifted with the special feature of thinking and imagining endlessly. It is this very feature that makes us superior to all the other organisms in this universe. The decisive power makes us think about good or bad. Also, notions of good and bad are part of our moral construct. To act good or bad is a matter of behaving in accordance or discordance with the established rules and rules are dynamic, they are not fixed. To prove that let's take an example from the past. The code of Hammurabi was written

b

To prove that let's take an example from the past. The code of Hammurabi was written by Hammurabi, a king who ruled

Mesopotamia. This code served as a cooperation manual for hundreds of thousands of people in his empire. It was a collection of several laws and judicial decisions whose aim was to present Hammurabi as a role model of a just king who would direct the land along the course of truth and correct way of life and teach future generations what justice is. According to him, people were divided into social hierarchies – Superiors, Commoners and Slaves. One of the rules written was that if a superior man blinds the eye or breaks the bone of another superior man, his eye shall be blinded and bone shall be broken whereas if a superior man does the same thing to a common or a slave man, h slave man, he shall pay a stipulated or pre-decided amount of silver. This kind of justice would obviously seem absurd and brazenly cruel or an act of barbarism and inequality to us, but in that era, Hammurabi was considered as the torchbearer of justice. But if this was considered good then, how can it be unacceptable now? This is because no event or occurrence is bad or good. Neither good nor bad is stagnant. Everything is relative, so is our thinking. I would like to conclude by saying that The fact that the viewpoints of people are changing constantly, shows that our classification of things as good and bad are based on our thinking, which is fluid and changes from time to time, depending on the forces of society.

12. ANJALI JHA

My name is Anjali Jha. I'm 13 years old. I like to write poems the most!

SELF BELIEF

Whenever I try to smile, people always knock in between.
Whenever I try to forget everything, I don't know why, they keep reminding me that I don't know anything.
But I have self belief, That I can touch the sky.
No matter what they say about me.
My confidence always makes me glee.
Whenever I tried to do something, they always demotivate me and tried to break my confidence.
But one day my success will give them answer that no one in this world is a loser.

13. DR SAIF ALI NAKHWA

Born and brought up in Mumbai, Dr Saif Ali Nakhwa is a medical graduate aspiring to be a good specialist and writer. An inquisitive bookworm, he loves to read anything and wants to know everything. An ardent devotee of The Divine Almighty, he strongly believes that he has been selected to serve humanity through medicine and literature. His Instagram username, calamus_gladius, in Latin, roughly means pen, sword. He is seriously 'An Inquisitive Freak And Literally Introverted'.

YOU ARE FINE. (BUT ARE YOU?)

He's someone who feels low
Cloth around neck, he often does twine
But is told, "Depression does not actually exist,
it's a myth, you are fine."
She's someone who panics a lot
A peaceful life she often does pineBut is told, "You are a
worrywart.
Stop being a total wuss, you are fine."
He's someone who desires guts

Despite having a morbid fear of swine
But is told "You are nothing
But a weakling, Grow up as you are fines."
She's someone who hates a mess
And compulsively sets things in line But is told, " You hard
nutcase,
stop Being a control freak, you are fine."
He's someone who eats a lot,
Always ready for a casual or fine dine.
But is told, " You aren't sick,
You just enjoy eating, so, you are fine."
She's someone who feels extremely low sometimes,
At times she's on a cloud higher than cloud nine.
But is told , " You're forging your madness as you
Wish to gather everyone's attention , you are fine.'
He's someone who lost his wife in a brutal crash.
He shudders everytime he sees the speed limit sign.
But is told, " Do not recall it and just move on
You're merely over reacting and therefore; you are fine."
She's someone who claims to hear voices
That tell her to starve, to make her soul shine.
But is told, " You're under arcane influence,
So exorcism is the only solution ; you are fine."
Society has ostracized people with mental disorders.
Taunting them , a lifelong stigma it does assign
It's time to help them and seek help if you have them,
As one may not be fine when told ," you are fine."

14. JANVI

Janvi, 18yrs old young writer. She has written several genres including thriller, horror, science fiction, epic fantasy, mystery and the list continues. Some of her famous works are:- Co-Author in EUPHORIA(Quill house Publication) , WANDERLUST(Write order publication) ,COMRADES (Samvn Publication) Winner of Halloween Hungama Event 2021 by scopup Magazine. Her contributions in the world of literature is her forthcoming projects. In this world of darkness, she want to enlighten the thoughts of many with the help of her writeups. These words are not merely her words. This is her VOICE..!! This is her FREEDOM..!!

ZEPHYR OF MEMORY

The best birthday ever, I'll remember that day forever Wingless sky suspended, above the garden of night With the blazing fiery embrace, There was a beauty even in murky enclasp I got a night full of stars, and wishes from flowers, The moon congratulates me, The spring breeze blessed me, I was singing with my loneliness, Dancing with my own shadows, Chatting with the enchanting sky, & felt like I can fly so high, And I love this way so much, cause, it has a comic touch, No cakes, no noises, Only me & the sky over the terrace No mold can shape as i quiver molten, Memories of best times are always frozen

15. TINA PATRICIA D'SOUZA

Tina Ptaricia D'Souza curently resides in Ontario, Canada with her husband. She is an auditor by profession and has worked with the Consulting and Financial Services Industries. In her spare time she likes volunteering towards causes such as mentorship, providing guidance to students and immigrants on work, education and job search. Reading, sketching and gardening and journaling her thoughts are some of her hobbies that she likes to indulge in. She has recently taken to getting her work published through poems and short stories and she hopes to pen down more.

MY MOULDING

I visualized myself of the woman i would be,
With the anticipation of leaving the familiar shores and anchoring at unkonwn territories,
With time, I have learnt lessons of patience, fortitude and the wisdom of age-old stories.
The hidden knowledge of a shooting star did I glean,
That one should not burn off in a blaze,

But glow bright with a beautiful glaze.
Self-asurance did I pick along the way,
Understanding that without him, it's so easy to sway.
Beauty in deed are the kind of acts in need,
Pearls of such wisdom I so often meet.
With my vision now adjusted,
I can't wait to make storms.
Making my 20's something
Laying the foundation for a legacy in my 30's
And making an impact in my 40's
Rearing to still go places in my 50's
And hopefully, still making eyes turn in my 60's
God willing, I won't stop at my 70's
I will still want to blaze even in my 80's
For i hope to be amazed at myself- at my silver hair and the
wrinkles achieved!
Travelling places, seeking wisdom
Gathering experiences and taking chances
With my portfolio thus complete,
I hope that my moulding will finally be replete.

16. PASUPULETI SRIVALLY

I started writing in my 8th standard. This is all because of my parents who support me a lot.

MY MEMORIES

My memories which are lagging behind me, I am not able to escape from them.

Trying to find the route but all are filled with thorns, evincing their revenge in a reality.

Whether the characteristics remain same but my memories make me think over.

Some memories are very strange but they make us know the truth.

Some memories are very happy at that moment. After many times of hurt they become our fault.

People usually don't remember their memories. If they really remember then they have to deserve all those.

But nowadays, forgetting our past memories make the person strong because,we are already hurt don't think of them which make you feel sad..

17. KHUSHI KUMARI

My name is Khushi. I'm 18 years old. I write poems and quotes on different genre such as fantasy, horror, fiction, non-fiction etc.My hobbies are reading books & writing. I love writing because it makes me feel free from inner stroms of heart. I think "Fantasy is better than reality!"

THE SKY SKETCH

When the sky is grey, it's going to rain,
When the sky is bright, everything's going to be alright.
When the sky starts raining, can't promise to control the dancing,
When the sky turns red, the heart fills with warmth and love.
When the sky gives a smile,the cheer on every face is high,
When the sky looks adorable, colourful butterflies start
wandering the sky.
When the sky is clear as crystal,it gives clear assurance of victory,
When the sky is blue,it indicates the wisdom inside you.
When the sky play with the winds, the bushes love to sway,
When the sky is painted with the rainbow, it says true friendship
never dies.

When the sky turns black at night, the twinkling stars shine over the darkness,
When the sky yawns in the nightfall, then there is no call.

18. ADITI TRIPATHI

My name is Aditi Tripathi. I was born on 12 April 2003. Right now I am a college student. I started writing when I was in twelfth standard and now writing is my heartful passion. It's my dream and goal to start an NGO for both humans and animals after starting my earnings. I love spirituality as it is a teaching of Spirit's Actuality. At last my sentence is , "There is some ITERNAL BLISS much more after worldly despute where soul explores the devinity."

THE PARADISE CHARM OF NATURE

The Brook , once I was passing by , rolling down the mountains ,but seems to be emerging from the heavens .
On The Union of Blue and Purple sky , Cotton Candy Clouds floating , and the Sun's Head looming , amidst the clouds , Like a Dome .
A playful Chubby Chipmunk , soaring-up a Tree , nibbling a nut , and chasing a Honey-bee .
The Carpet of green-grass , laid by the creation , and the , Natural Vases Of colourful majestic flowers , Sown inside the lap

*of , mother nature. This captivating , paradise picturesque ,
designed by the angel creators , stuck the sight , solace the mind .
-Aditi Tripathi ©groovyangel*

• 31 •

19. RIA BANERJEE

Hi, I am Ria, an avid reader and a budding poet, have been published as a poet and short story writer, love long walks and tea.

Garden of Temptation

They made her out of my rib, They wanted me to be happy.
They said she would fill me with joy, show me wonder and ultimate bliss.
She came, I saw her mesmerised, She looked at me, her eyelashes fluttered.
A snake underneath the cloak of a helpless feline, she beckoned, I followed, wondering after her, blinded by lust, She led ahead, her body swayed, like an apple tree laden with fruits.
I knew not where she took me, blinded by her, I followed.
She ushered me in the world of knowledge, A world of pain and surrender. No longer was ignorance a bliss, My eyes opened up, realized that world was pandora's box, Happiness was just an illusion, Pain and sorrow were a reality,
I cursed and bewailed my fate. Damned as I was, forever, by the garden of temptation.

20. ANANYA YEASMIN

Ananya Yeasmin is a school student. Writing has always been her passion. Presently, her writing got published in few anthologies.

NEVER PUT PINEAPPLE ON PIZZA!

Aditya could hardly keep his eyes open, but sleep was far away even though he tried very hard. He kept tossing and turning, thinking about the dream he got last night. He saw a wolf whose eyes were full of mystery, heading towards him. It jumped forward to attack him. With intense fear, he woke up and jumped out of his bed. He was sweating profusely. He spilled his coffee on his shirt this morning. He couldn't concentrate on his work too, and on his way home, he took the wrong bus. Getting home was troublesome, as he had to travel two hours more to return from that unfamiliar route. He has never been so distracted before. "Ugh, the day was a complete mess." He sighed. Just then, he heard a knock against the window panes. He opened it but saw nothing, so he was going back to his bed, when he heard it again. It was louder this time. He stepped out of his house from the backdoor to check what exactly was happening. To his terror, he saw a wolf h

. To his terror, he saw a wolf hitting the panes with its paw. Aditya watched it carefully and realised that it's eyes were mysterious, just like the wolf in his dreams. He turned pale in fear and was shivering, when the wolf turned around and ran. Aditya felt a strange urge to follow. He followed the wolf until he disappeared into darkness. He turned on the flashlight of his phone and continued to walk, but he couldn't see the wolf anywhere. All he could see were tall trees. There was a canopy of the massive leaves above him, preventing even a bit of moonlight to enter the ground. He was puzzled as he had neither seen nor heard anything about here. Moreover it's strange for a forest with wild animals like wolves to be there in the middle of the city. There was a very tall and thick tree, with a large opening on it. He stepped inside. Darkness gulped him and to add to the hassle, his phone died. All of a sudden, there was an unforeseen flash of light with a loud booming voice coming from with a loud booming voice coming from every direction. "Do you like pineapple on pizza?" "Umm, why?" Aditya stuttered. "Your answer will determine your fate" "Am I dead? Will this decide whether I can enter paradise or not?" "Don't ask questions to me!" The voice grew deeper. "No, how can I die so early, that too a virgin!!?" "Huh, that's what his main concern is. Answer my question, young man!" "What about the ten commandments?" "That's old. It's 2021. Now tell me your answer." "To be honest, I do like pineapple on pizza. Yeah okay, I am a psychopath, I agree." Suddenly a massive door appeared infront of him. "Go on.", The voice uttered. The crumbling edges and the husky panels begged him to enter. As soon as he did, he felt like he was falling into a bottomless pit. He closed his eyes out of fear and jumped out of his bed just like he did, the previous day. It was morning already. "Phew! It was a dream. Thank God.", He sighed and went to the bathroom to freshen up, but to his horror, his

He sighed and went to the bathroom to freshen up, but to his horror, his face was filled with hair. It resembled the face of a wolf. He screamed his throat out and then there was that loud, husky voice again. "Welcome to the world of nightmares, young man! Your dreams come to life here. Enjoy your stay, because you're not leaving.....Never!"

21. PIPAVATH SURAJ

I'm PIPAVATH SURAJ studing graduation final year. I am from Telangana State, Dist:Nizamabad from India.

One day a man and an ant carrying loads on their shoulders were walkig on the road. Suddenly man fell on his knees due to heavy load, as he found none who came to help, he himself stood and sat under a tree. Surprisingly he noticed a group of ants that came to help the ant which felt down due to heavy load. When he asked the ant about this the it replied that our hands might be small but we always offer a helping hand when someone is in need and that is much bigger than you think, Humans might fail to show humanity but we and other animals never fail to show that.

Moral : The true wealth is unity and humanity.

- Surya.

22. CRUMPLED PAPERBALLS

Namaste, I'm crumpled paperballs. I'm a 19 year old budding writer who started off with writing BTS fanfictions last year. Exploring people's mind is what I want to pen down. Notepad is my safe place. As a BTS's ARMY, I'd say that always live life on your own terms, help people as much as you can and always take care of your physical and mental health. Every single individual matters a lot to a lot? Spread love?

In the middle of the night, Taewook sits on the floor near his bedside table. Under the dim yellow light of a rusty brown lamp, he opens his diary and starts scribbling a long note. Dear Jungwan Since when have you become so stubborn? Tsk... Wan... I made you your favourite marble cupcakes two days ago. You must have seen them in the fridge. It's kinda surprising that the plate is still untouched. Hmm... I wonder how angry can you be with me! I remember you saying, "You are the most endearing and desirable boy I've ever seen." And every single time, I'd purse my lips to stop smiling at your lustful glance. Then I'd look away to hide the flushed cheeks of mine, in response to which you'd kiss me like there's no tomorrow. Yeah, I'm being impatient. I can wait no longer to feel your fingertips tracing my sensitive spine, arching more and more with every warm touch of yours. I love the way you demarcate your boundaries on the land you already own, with purplemspots of pure affection. "I'll be gentle" you say before proceeding to wreck this keyhole with just the perfect key of yours. Pecking my pounding chest till pleasure overrides the pain can never fail to work on me, indeed. Wan.. I really miss you.. Your voice, as deep as your sea green eyes, rings in my ears every now and again. I come running into our room with a hope to talk to you, to apologise for whatever happened that night.. But you... You just lie on the bed, unbothered by my presence. Ceiling appeals you a lot nowadays, isn't it? I can't stand seeing you like this. I know that the things turned really ugly that night but... I promise, I'll make it alright. Goodnight babe Love you. With that, he closes his diary. After switching off the lamp, he stands up and lies on the bed beside Jungwan. Turning to his side, he mumbles, "Close your eyes, wan. It's time to sleep. Here, let me help you." He shuts his stiffened eyelids with his palm to stop him from staring at the ceiling. Then he carefully tilts his head towards his side and studies every inch of his face, lovingly. Pulling up the blood soaked blanket over his husband's shoulder, he covers himself partially with the same. He snuggles into his bloodied neck, unbothered by the slit throat. Though the butcher knifes piercing through Jungwan's stomach weren't letting the blanket cover his cold and Taewook's warm body properly, but any of them hardly cared about it. Arguments, fights, dried blood or the suffocating smell, nothing can keep Taewook from loving his husband. "Sleep well babe.." he whispers under his breath, before closing his eyes.

23. ANMEET CHAWLA

Hello, my name is Anmeet. I started writing during my school days. At first I used to write quotes and articles, but with my improving English, I started writing poetry. Last Photograph is one of the first stories that I wrote, I hope it speaks out to my readers and they will appreciate it.

Last Photograph

"The most pleasing sounds never sustain and the most beautiful thing can never be photographed", would've been my last thoughts, before reality had taken over. Well, it's fall season in Canada before I'm ought to leave for Scotland, next week. I've been in Canada for a couple of weeks only realising how different cultures can get when we wound up with some thousands of miles, after all I'm a photographer and I love to watch. Unlike the usual Canadians, who are obviously busy pertaining to Thanksgiving, I'm going to the countryside, which I want to explore and probably it can help me calm down after being under these absorbing days.

Cardigans and frosts are old friends who tend to come closer with every incoming Autumn day. The sky is clear unlike the path which I'm on, which is filled with maple leaves that are rustling with every passing of my leather step above them. I had to clean my camera lens as the mist wasn't the only thing but the charms surrounding me were forcing me to capture that fantasy every now and then. After walking quite a bit, I came across a beautiful sight just beside a pond, to get a vivid view of those ducks, which I could hear harking from afar. Reaching the edge of the pond, I glimpsed upon a black-haired beauty, who was feeding those birds. Usually, I capture essence around me, but this time, those two hazel eyes, captured the realm inside me. "Good afternoon!", I said, "Good afternoon", she replied in that faint echo, which took over the silence all around me, for a second. "I'm Aaron, I was passing through the woods, when I saw you feeding these ducks", I said. "Hi, I'm Valerie, it's Hi, I'm Valerie, it's just one of my daily routines out here", said Valerie in a joyful mood. After some healthy conversations with Valerie, and probably setting my eye's focus on manual mode, I was glancing at that surreal visage a lot more, than I was hearing whatever she was saying to me. "I'm new to this area, that's why I'm becoming an explorer day by day", chuckled Valerie. She told me that she lived in a nearby manor just past the pond. She gave an uneasy, long stare at the camera I was carrying as if she was one of my lost camera reels, which I've just found. While I was lost in this made-up fantasy of mine, I couldn't help, but notice Valerie making unusual girly poses at a nearby tree as if she was reckoning me to click her. The breeze was sharp and cold, but the presence of Valerie made me feel as if every flurry gust was giving me moist and warm hugs from her.

Being obedient to my passion, I started clicking her photographs, until, the brumous sunset, made me realize that t
her photographs, until, the brumous sunset, made me realize that the surreal scenery surrounding us was nothing, in front of those two captivating hazel islands in their respective white lakes. "Ah, it's quite late now, I should get back to town", I said to her. "I'll be on my way too", said Valerie to me. I think it was just my destiny or a developing tryst between us, that made me say, "If you don't have a problem, can I walk you to your manor?". "All right, sure!", she said, and the swiveling of the wind past her hair, kind of assured my question. We started walking towards her manor and it was quite some time when we reached there. I could see nothing past a mile or so, as the mist was quite up now, so was the dusk. Her manor looked like a royal building and I was gettin

We started walking towards her manor and it was quite some time when we reached there. I could see nothing past a mile or so, as the mist was quite up now, so was the dusk. Her manor looked like a royal building and I was getting the vibes as if I was in the Victorian era. It was strange for such a big house to be in the middle of nowhere. We greeted and the moment I was about to leave, she said, "Aaron, can you click a last photograph of me with my manor?". A sudden sustained echo started fading my brain and just when I was about to say something to her, I fell unconscious.

"I think I'm okay, it's really dark now that's why I can't see a thing", I comforted myself, while my hands were busy feeling the

forest floor. I could hear but can't see, the sirens and some people murmuring and inspecting the area around where I was lying. "They would be some forest rangers of that area", I thought. "Roger that, sir, we have found him", I heard a ranger saying. I felt someone handcuffing me while I kept on screaming, "Why are you doing this to me? Please switch on the torch, I want to see around".It seemed like an unreal reality, I was back in. A ranger then yelped into my ear, "It's the fifth time, you've managed to flee from your cell in the asylum, you idiot blind man!". "Which cell? Which asylum

Which asylum? Why can't I see the manor? I'm a photogr....", I tried my useless screams in that pitch dark. The tears started rolling down my cheeks which made me realize that I was blind. I started fumbling my hands on those dew-soaked maples around me to find my camera, but there was nothing. "Where is my camera?", I cried, "Oh, it's his same story again, shut him up!", freaked one of the rangers, tightening his hand's grip on me. It was about time when I realized I wasn't any photographer and was recognized as a mentally unstable man, living in that asylum, which the rangers told me was previously a manor, for over fifty years. The only camera I once possessed were my eyes, after all, she was the last photograph I ever captured through them, fifty years ago.

24. GAURAV BANERJEE

An aspiring writer who wants to publish his own novel. HR assistant by day and a writer by night.

"I wish I could leave you my love, but my heart is a mess" played on her playlist as she gathered courage and not knowing exactly where to go, she headed to the local train station intent on going somewhere. "Ticket please", said the lady with a deliberate tone. "Where to Mam?" replied the clerk. "Anywhere but here", said the lady with a nod.

"Well those tickets are a bit expensive!" replied the clerk. The lady looked at the clerk perplexed, but she was dead set on being anywhere except where she was. "Very well then, how much is it?" "I'm afraid it will cost everything you have," replied the clerk cautiously. The lady was feeling agitated at this point. She pened up her wallet, pulled out all of the bills, and slapped them on the ticket counter. "That's all I have. Will it be enough?" "If that's all you have, then it will do," replied the clerk handing the lady a ticket. The lady looked down at the ticket with disdain. She grunted, "Why this is the plainest and most ordinary ticket I've

ever seen. For the most expensive ticket available, you'd at least think it would be something special!"

The clerk smiled compassionately. He then called out as the lady walked away, "We have two loading tracks, Mam. The first is for the hourly train. The second leaves once a day at noon. You'll be looking for the noon train on the second track." The lady nodded and made her way to the loading area. She was shocked to see how many people were already there waiting for the same train.

She found an open seat on a bench next to a middle-aged woman and sat down. "So where are you headed?" she asked. "Anywhere but here," the woman responded matter-of-factly. "Right, right. Of course," the lady replied looking down at her ticket. A few hours later, the lady found herself comfortably aboard the train, enjoying a hot cup of tea, and gazing out the window. She was looking forward to finally being anywhere but where she was. However, as the hours whizzed by as fast as the landscape outside, she became antsy. Exasperated, she tapped a passenger on the shoulder and asked, "Excuse me, sir, how long have we been on this train? Shouldn't we have arrived by now?" The passenger, barely breaking his gaze out the window, replied, "How long? I suppose I've been traveling for about a year now." The lady was fuming at this point. "Is that why the tickets are so expensive? Because people end up riding for so long?" "Yes, I suppose that is part of it. But it always costs a lot when you decide to be somewhere other than where you are." "Above every seat runs a pull-cord. To get off, all you have to do is simply give the pull-cord two sharp tugs and the train will let you off. It was part of your on-boarding instructions." "Oh," said the lady with a slight surprise. "I guess I wasn't paying attention." She jumped over the back of her seat, grabbed her knapsack, and gave two deliberate yanks on the pull-cord. The train immediately began to slow. The brakes squealed and finally hissed with relief as the train shuttered to a stop.

She leaped out of the door and hit the ground running. She ran deep into the middle of an open meadow, one that would have flashed by in the blink of an eye had she still be on the train. With arms thrust into the air she shouted, "I want to be here! I want to be here!" It was the middle of nowhere, but for the first time in her life, she was somewhere. And it felt so good to be there. "To sway like it was Friday night and all the lights will blind me dry" made so much sense now.

25. GRAHEET SHENOY

"This is where all these whores belong", he slurs pointing at his crotchal area precisely towards his junk again and again as if to make sure that his companion for the eve takes clear notice to what he is pointing at. Though this was completely unnecessary as the whole bar had their undivided attention to this drunk man and his liquor-act; eyes glued onto him somewhat akin to the silence perpetuated by a major wardrobe malfunction bestowed upon by the universe on an unfortunate 2nd grader in a well-crowded school play. The waiter trotted towards the scene confused whether to hold this stumbling falling man or to call someone to throw him out and rid him of this misery. As the waiter approached nearer, the 'friend' of the man in question, the company, (presumably in this case a right man at the wrong time, as this 'friend' was no kin of the drunkard but a mere stranger who had been chosen to be a part of this debauchery completely unwilling) beckoned him not get any closer as no one knows what might trigger this creature into more scornful actions. The 'friend' then fused the situation by holding the drunk mess up by his hand and then to his chair.

The ruckus had been on for quite a while now, way before the nuisance had even set foot in the bar. The dipsomaniac was an artist apparently, a theatre artist. From Macbeth to the caesar, Hamlet to Lear, he had been stabbed, cheated on, neglected, swindled, betrayed over and over for almost about 21 years now, right from when he was 8 and had for the first time played the role of a pillar that cracks and breaks away when Hiranyakashpu strikes it with all his might fretted by his son's devotion over other gods, in a skit that was organised by the unemployed lads supporting the municipal councilor in an occasion for Ganesh Chaturti.

This alliance between the 'friend' and the liquor breath-man was abetted sheerly by pity at the plight of his hopelessness: A strange man, completely intoxicated approaching a random person(the 'friend') and babbling with great pride "An artist is like water, transparent….. embodying the shape of anything the world puts us into…… and… they… they make me do.. This…THIS.!!" before almost fainting and ironically asking for water with his dry, dehydrated and simmering voice. Awoke, fortunately the next bright day right at his doorsteps with a sharp pain on the upper back of his neck and a nasty hangover, he glides his hands flailing through each one of his trouser pockets in search of a lighter to light a thrown half cigarette stub he had just found on the pavement.

He tries to recollect the incidents that had conspired the night before. Unfortunately, everything after his squabble with the director who was also the owner of the theatre he worked at, was vague and hazy. As he wakes up with the support of the banister next to him, fused with a head rush he is reminded of a complete stranger but with no recollection of his face, whom he had befriended somewhere along his bender and was convinced that this human form of an angel had promptly delivered him to his doorsteps in the middle of the night. He thrusts his hand into his jeans through his inner garments toward his shin to inspect if anything was missing or had been fiddled with, but other than an unwelcome erection which was pushed to make a breatheeasy space; the goods seemed intact. He let out a sigh as according to him anyone could easily take advantage of a man these days as the world was now filled with only cheating whores and thieving faggots.

faggots. A random stranger who had not only not picked his pocket but also dropped his unconscious self back home unharmed could only in his thinking be categorized into something non existing for this v world - a devine entity. Dejected and nonchalant, he makes his way to the bed knowing very well that he is pushed again in all swing, back to the same place he was toiling in before : bottom of a well called unemployment. He throws himself on his cot like a lifeless corpse and sinks into a deep slumber. The new theatre gig in the city was for his sake a resuscitation. Even though he had somewhat of a decent stature back in his hometown with a recognisable amount of fanship in the nearby villages, all thanks to the drama tours and Harikathe plays he had indulged himself in; The city seemed to have no such facilitation waiting for him and treated him nothing better than hundreds of other talented artists waiting for a break.

While back in his place he was a shining dew drop reflecting the dawn's first sun rays after a rainy night, here he was nothing but a speck of drop in a raining storm of artists. He had to even scrape toilets and clean streets for a day's meal at a point. Lonely nights were haunted by the memories of his old life of fame and respect which had been shattered by a riot mob that decided to burn down the one theatre in the entire village that only ever premiered Shakesphere plays with an accusation attached of not promoting the vernacular. Even though the plays were never in English but actually an adaptation translated verbatim and performed in the local dialect, the rioters believed that this overshadowed numerous important artships passed from generations to the next in the local language and left hundreds of families starving, jobless, who did not understand the tone and how to act in a foriegn play.

play. He was pushed to the city inevitably like thousand others in search of ways to fill his stomach. It was a stifling, famishing struggle until his talents were finally recognized by a director through the word of mouth of a friend who had learnt of this striving artist's past from another friend. The director liked him straight away and took the man in with open arms, providing him with a dingy but sufficient place to stay and also handed him with a decent concession to get him back on his feet. But how could an artist with such aptitude who had captivated people of all ages purely with his talents in his prime be given a *role so demeaning, a role so fruitless and talentless, a role of a luscious woman, the manipulating slow poison of the society. Out of all the roles that should have brought him honor and fame, this was by far the worst. He was once as a kid given the role of a tree, a bloody tree that did nothing so to speak, and he still considered this, to play a woman, his com considered this, to play a woman, his complete low. His affection toward women as he himself has shared a couple of times was that of a man's toward his pet dog. The dog no matter how close to one's heart can be allowed free for a while and roam around but the moment it starts being too friendly it must be punished and disciplined to be put back in its place. Had someone asked him 2 months before when he had first been given the role in the play as to what he felt about acting as a woman on the stage, he would have shrugged and thrown at them proudly the women-pet analogy which he had come up with all by himself. But now, not so much, now not so clear, now not so sure.*

The play was of 90 minutes stretch, with a short break in the middle. 3 shows a day for two days a week, the weekends. Now the play itself was quite simple, a woman in her 20's, mesmerizingly beautiful (as much as a human with male features can be made up to look) is travelling back to her home along her usual commute. But one grave day she is abducted by four of her co-workers as she had once been hostile towards one of them lashing back at him for having continually tormented her stating his attraction and love for her. They, then force themselves on her bound body one by one, leaving her raped naked

trembling cold unconscious corpse stranded in a pool of blood
and tears; at which point the play ends and the curtain drops.
He was at first set a little aback about the request of playing a
woman's role, but as his own lips had spoken "Artists are but
water" and so to do justice to his words and to heed his crying
stomach, he was up and ready, ready to do this and be done with
it. How h

How hard could it be? A woman after all. Just a thieving,
manipulating, lust filled woman. A woman who whored around
so much, who had played around with so many other men's lives
that she got herself raped by her own colleagues. "I bet she even
enjoyed it. Being ploughed by 4 aroused men, that's what she
wanted anyway right?. That's what women do.. She asked for it
and she got it.. Just a little crocodile tears to act coy at the end…
women are something… aren't they?.. Lord!!, he spoke to himself
when he was told about his character in the play. The director
wanted to bring out a sort of rough and improvised way of
dialogue rendering and hence had only explained the plot of the
play, the basic storyline and had asked the actors to immerse
themselves into their respective character's mindsets, without
handing them a script of any sort.
A lot of scrupulous examining and screening had been put into
the selection process of these fine actors and he knew he must not
chain their artistic spirits to a piece of paper. But on the first day
of rehearsals he did hand them each over with a written copy of
dialogues, not detailed but more like an exoskeleton, "Just a
blueprint which needed cement, bricks and rods with beams and

pillars to build a skyscraper of a show.", he had said. To the astonishment of our problematic booze-barrel, his role of the young fleshy woman who he had thought her to be asking, tempting and teasing the young men to the extent of mauling her like sex-raged boars, was actually a kattar subservient muslim. Which meant that she had never touched a drop of alcohol, offered her salat everyday, attended hajj and paid her homage to the holy Mecca atleast once every four years. And also she wore her hijab, she covered her precious body from the eyes of evil. Is it irony or tragedy? She never asked for it. She did not reveal anything to woo these poor men on the stand. What made her co-workers inflict pain onto a person while looking at her come to work daily under a burka paying her respects to the lord everyday lawfully even when she was drowning in heaps of work? What kind of bad deed had she committed to have met with such barbaric fate? These were the thoughts that reverberated around the whole day in the artist's head. But he brushed these mysteries off for the moment. He would not let these questions ruin his performance or even a single second of his peace. He shook them all off and went about, to give a heartfelt portrayal of his character. But these questions, these were boulders, boulders that stormed onto the thought puddle of his brain and struck each and every nerve. Dug deep and demanded answers. They did not disrupt his acting as he had thought, they actually empowered it. Filled his act with right emotions. Made it convincing. It was only now that the ice was finally melting, the ice was turning into water, the water that embodies all the containers of the world, the water that the artist himself had spoken of before. The rehearsals and the plays went on for hours and then days which turned into weeks. Weeks and weeks of him racking his brain trying to figure out, what? Just what? Did she do wrong? How was the poor innocent in any way wrong? way wrong? What should she have done better? What could she have done better? She kept to her work. Did not hurt a soul. Had God in her heart, then why? why? why is she being punished? Is this the fate of every women in this world? He couldn't find a moment of peace. He could not sleep anymore, he felt as if he woke up daily, freshened up just to go get stripped naked on the stage in front of everyone. His fellow artists undressing him on the stage, the audience's lustrous eyes tearing his apparels, piercing through his bare skin. He would get ready, get dressed, get raped and go back, not sleep, get dressed and get raped again and again. This was his new life. He couldn't find a shred of hope to keep going. He felt as if everyone was watching him all the time, on or off the stage. He had started noticing the eyes, hundreds of eyes, just staring, thousands of eyes with lust staring everywhere he went. These eyes that stare, they have always been staring, they have been staring at every women of every age, of every culture and every religion, nothing mattered, what one wore, how one behaved, how good or bad they were, if even a little bit of flesh was visible these eyes would stare. How were they hidden from his vicinity till now? These many years he had survived on this ugly wide earth and how had he not once seen them? These monstrous eyes that stare while waiting on a bus, that stare at a vegetable market, that stare on their students, their maids, their relatives, their mothers and their sisters, no one seemed safe for the oppression of eyes. He was drained from within, estranged from his soul, stranded so far away, he could see no return.

Until one day he couldn't keep it all in. He started pouring it out, broke down right in the middle of the play on the stage. The director who confused this for an exuberant act almost teared at the sensational performance, until the man had missed his cue to stop and had not seized his sobs even after the curtain was down. The director was now genuinely concerned trotted closer to the torn artist and put his hand on the man's shoulder as a comfort.

The actor jolted the director's hands away, roared at him, screamed and stormed out of the room. Sipping on his liquor flask he rushed towards the road and started walking aimlessly, which had been the genesis of his alcohol filled bender which then had led to him into a bar with a stranger('the friend'), create a scene, and had landed him on the threshold of his door and now on his bed hungover, unconscious and probably unemployed.

unemployed. The doorbell rang once, twice and thrice. After a pause, on having no response whatsoever, there came an alarming continuous bang on the door. This struck the artist plunging out of the bed with a murderous headache. He looked at his pillow which was soaking wet, he had cried in his sleep again. He picked up a towel lying on the floor to wipe the moist off his face and flipped the wet side of the pillow down. He *inched towards the door and opened it, it was the maid. As soon as he opened the door ,she channeled her gaze towards the bottom of the door hinge waiting for the routine string of taunts and insults and to ignore it all and get to her work as usual. But nothing happened today, the man just manufactured a slight smile, let the maid in and went right to his bed and then into a placid nap.*

26. VIRAJ JOSHI

Viraj Joshi (He/She/They) is a second year student at the University of Delhi graduating in English. Tenacious is the word that describes him the best. He believes there are 101 ways of doing great in life and writing is one among them. His favorite quote is from The Bhagavad Gita which reads, 'Change is the law of the universe. You can be a millionaire, or a pauper in an instant.'

LOST IN EVOCATION!

When the darkness of the night was quiet and while multitudinous thoughts crossed my mind, I decided to scroll my playlist, and then all of a sudden, your effigy walloped me. I harked back to, how every weekend we used to lie down at my patio, with your hand in mine, and tried chanting each other's dearest lyrics. how we got accustomed to sharing our repast followed by confectioneries in school during every day's recess and you would childishly voice, "I want a big portion, otherwise, I will not eat ".

eat ". how we both concluded to choose Economics as the same optional subject so that we need not part away for even those 45 odd minutes. how you used to enunciate, "People watching" and then I would hug you even tighter after every date. how every morning you got habituated to confirm with me, "Coming to school?" and then validate back in a dismal tone, "Viraj, not coming?", if I'd revert with a NO. I recalled, I recalled it all. I craved for, one time, one last time, If I could link up to you and mayhap make you notice, I wasn't bad..., Just couldn't prove...!!!

Lost in evocation, I adjusted my pillow, rested my head against it, And caroled the words of your favorite lyric, ...There goes my heart beating 'Cause you are the reason I'm losing my sleep Please come back now.... Love, to the extra special one!... Period!!

27. ANJALI SINGH

*I am a native of Hariyagara village in Gonda district , U.p.
Interested in reading as well as writing quotes , poetry , short
stories and shayaris Preferred language:- English and Hindi
Topic of interest:- Romance and motivation I find writing as the
best option to express all my thoughts or feelings On a way to
build a beautiful future "A simple girl with unique thoughts."*

तुम गलत नहीं हो।

तुम याद करो ना करो,
वो तुम्हारी वफ़ा या बेवफ़ाई होगी।
हो सकता है तुम्हारे साथ भी
किसी ने मोहब्बत नही निभाई होगी।

या फिर ये भी हो सकता है कि कुछ,
मजबूरियों ने ये दूरियां बढ़ाई होगी
या फिर तुमने वो सारी कसमें ही झूटी खाई होंगी।

लेकीन इतने भी पत्थर दिल नही हो तुम, जानते हैं हम
कि जिस दिन हम रोए थे इतना,
आंखें तुम्हारी भी जरूर भर आई होंगी।

हम जानते हैं तुम नही हो गलत,
गलत तो हम भी नही हैं मेरी जान।
लेकिन हम खुदको ही गलत कह देंगे सबसे,
वरना ज़माने में तुम्हारी ही रुसवाई होगी।